LIFE IN HELL

WITH LOVE FROM HELL

FOR THE MAN WHO UNDERSTANDS....

WITH LOVE FROM HELL

HELL SWEET HELL

WITH LOVE FROM HELL

LIFE IN HELL

WITH LOVE FROM HELL

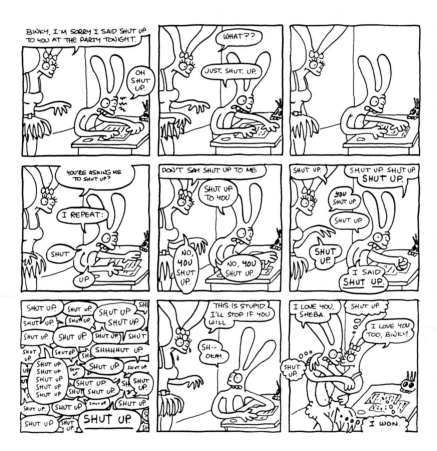

WITH LOVE FROM HELL

LIFE IN
HELL

FROM THE DESK OF BONGO

BONGO'S LOVE LETTERS (NEVER SENT)

DEAR SNARLA, I ♥ you. Anonymus

OH SNARLA, I REALLY ♥ you. Anonymus

♥ you DESPARATELY. Anonymus

BONGO'S FORGED EXCUSE

Please excuse Bongo from his absense yester day. He had a terribel ear ache.
Bongo's Daddy

PORTRAIT OF MOM

SELF-PORTRAIT

PORTRAIT OF DAD

BONGO'S LETTER TO SANTA

Dear Santa,
All I want for Xmas is my two front teeth.
And another ear.
Your freind,
Bongo

PORTRAIT OF BEST FRIEND

BONGO'S HOMEWORK

I am a bad Bongo.
I am a bad Bongo.
I am a bad Bongo.
I am a bad Bongo.
I am a bad Bongo.
I am a bad Bongo.

WITH LOVE FROM HELL

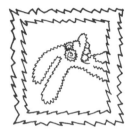

WITH LOVE FROM HELL

LIFE IN HELL

© 1989 BY
MATT
GROENING

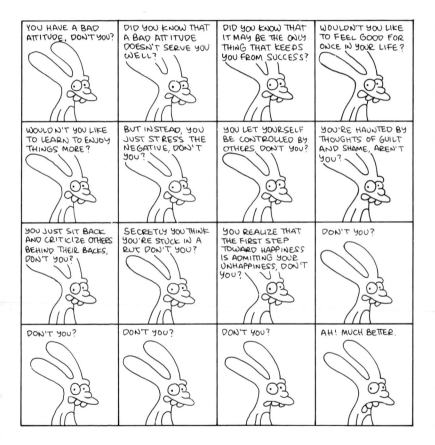

WITH LOVE FROM HELL

LIFE IN HELL

WITH LOVE FROM HELL

A STRIP CALLED
HELL

©1984
BY MATT
GROENING

YOUR FAVORITE T-SHIRT REVEALS YOUR PERSONALITY

WITH LOVE FROM HELL

LIFE IN HELL

IS LOVE HELL?

WITH LOVE FROM HELL

HOT & STEAMY
LIFE
IN
HELL

WITH LOVE FROM HELL

LIFE IN HELL

WITH LOVE FROM HELL

THINKING OF U...

WITH LOVE FROM HELL

LIFE IN HELL

THE MANY MOODS OF BINKY

WITH LOVE FROM HELL

LIFE IN HELL

WITH LOVE FROM HELL

LIFE IN HELL

THE MANY MOODS OF SHEBA

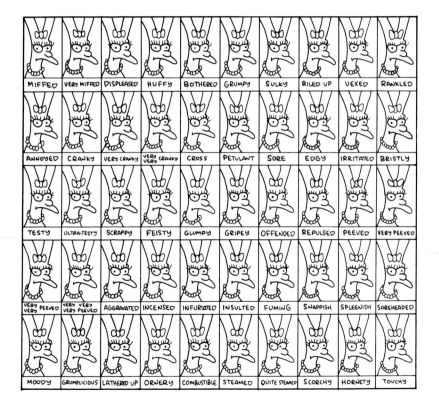

WITH LOVE FROM HELL

© 1991 by Matt Groening Productions, Inc. · HarperPerennial · Use first class postage

WITH LOVE FROM HELL

THE 24 STAGES OF SEXUAL AROUSAL

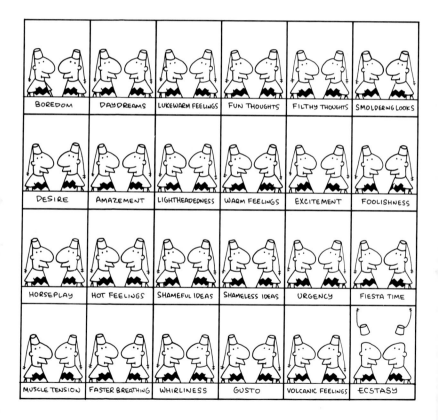

WITH LOVE FROM HELL

BASIC SEX FACTS FOR TODAY'S YOUNGFOLK

FOR GIRLS ONLY

REMEMBER PLAYING WITH YOUR FAVORITE TOY WHEN YOU WERE A LITTLE KID? WELL, SEX IS EVEN BETTER.

WHEN AUTHORITIES WARN YOU OF THE SINFULNESS OF SEX, THERE IS AN IMPORTANT LESSON TO BE LEARNED. DO NOT HAVE SEX WITH THE AUTHORITIES.

FIG. 1
THE BOY

SOMEDAY EVEN YOU WILL SLEEP WITH ONE.

[IF GAY, SEE FIG. 2]

MASTURBATION IS NOTHING TO BE ASHAMED OF. IT'S NOTHING TO BE PARTICULARLY PROUD OF, EITHER.

YOUR SEX LIFE WILL IMPROVE IMMENSELY AS SOON AS YOU MOVE AWAY FROM YOUR PARENTS.

FOR A GOOD TIME, GET A PARTNER WHO WILL ACT AS RIDICULOUS AS YOU.

IS IT TRUE THAT BOYS ARE AS OBSESSED WITH SEX AS GIRLS ARE? YES YES YES. THEY HAVE EVEN BEEN KNOWN TO SNEAK PEEKS AT EXPRESSLY FORBIDDEN SEX FACTS MARKED "FOR GIRLS ONLY."

FOR BOYS ONLY

REMEMBER PLAYING WITH YOUR FAVORITE TOY WHEN YOU WERE A LITTLE KID? WELL, SEX IS EVEN BETTER.

WHEN AUTHORITIES WARN YOU OF THE SINFULNESS OF SEX, THERE IS AN IMPORTANT LESSON TO BE LEARNED. DO NOT HAVE SEX WITH THE AUTHORITIES.

FIG. 2
THE GIRL

SOMEDAY EVEN YOU WILL SLEEP WITH ONE.

[IF GAY, SEE FIG. 1]

MASTURBATION IS NOTHING TO BE ASHAMED OF. IT'S NOTHING TO BE PARTICULARLY PROUD OF, EITHER.

YOUR SEX LIFE WILL IMPROVE IMMENSELY AS SOON AS YOU MOVE AWAY FROM YOUR PARENTS.

FOR A GOOD TIME, GET A PARTNER WHO WILL ACT AS RIDICULOUS AS YOU.

IS IT TRUE THAT GIRLS ARE AS OBSESSED WITH SEX AS BOYS ARE? YES YES YES. THEY HAVE EVEN-- AW, YOU GET THE PICTURE.

WITH LOVE FROM HELL

LIFE IN HELL

WITH LOVE FROM HELL

THE HELL WITH YOU

WITH LOVE FROM HELL

LIFE IN HELL

WITH LOVE FROM HELL

LIFE IN HELL

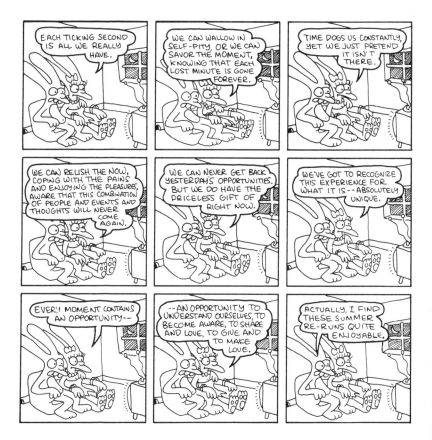

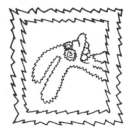

WITH LOVE FROM HELL

LIFE IN HELL

THE 24 WARNING SIGNS OF STRESS

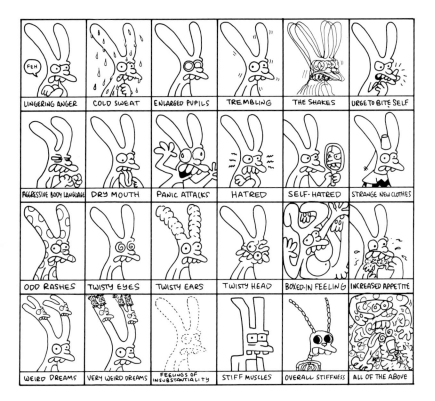

WITH LOVE FROM HELL

LIFE IN HELL

WITH LOVE FROM HELL

IS LOVE HELL?

WITH LOVE FROM HELL

WITH LOVE FROM HELL

WITH LOVE FROM HELL

LIFE IN HELL

HOW MUCH STRESS IS TOO MUCH STRESS?

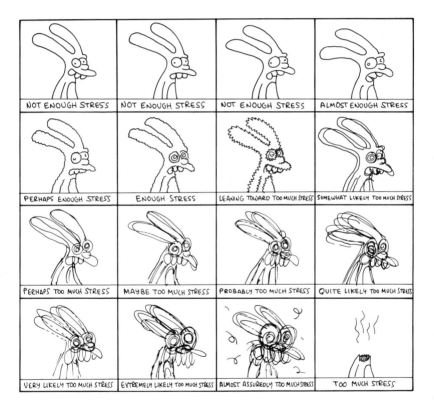

WITH LOVE FROM HELL

LIFE IN HELL

WITH LOVE FROM HELL

LIFE IN HELL

WITH LOVE FROM HELL